TA
A Study of The First Six
Chapters of the Book of Daniel

By Frank Beck
&
Patricia Chadwick

Chuck,

To my good friend in ministry.

Frank

Copyright © 2003
Frank Beck & Patricia Chadwick

All Rights Reserved

ISBN 0-9709123-5-8

Published 2003

Published by P.C. Publications, 22 Williams St., Batavia, NY 14020, USA ©2002 Frank Beck and Patricia Chadwick. All rights reserved. No part of this publication may be reproduced, stored in a retrieval system, or transmitted in any form or by any means, electronic, mechanical, recording or otherwise, without the prior written permission of the author.

Manufactured in the United States of America.

P.C. Publications, Inc.
2003

3

TAKING A STAND
A Study of The First Six Chapters of the Book of Daniel

Frank Beck & Patricia Chadwick

Dedication

To my wife, Zelma Beck. I find myself forever grateful for this extraordinary woman who has made life so special because she has been there day after day. Zelma is my hero and I don't say that to her enough. Thank you dear for being such a faithful partner in ministry.

Table of Contents

Acknowledgements

When you have been preaching for over forty years and twenty-five of those years have been at the same church, you begin to wonder about preaching. I know that scripture is very clear about "preach the Word", but I wonder, even as I preach under the anointing of the Lord—could God use this even more if a broader audience heard the Word, too? And would it have a greater affect if people had time to sit with the Word and meditate and contemplate over it which a book form would afford them that opportunity? After forty years of preaching I have been moved to put some of my sermon series in book form and see if God could use them in a greater way to His honor and glory. This small book is the beginning of this adventure. If it helps you in any way, may the Lord be praised.

I must thank Patti Chadwick for prodding me on in this adventure of putting some of my sermons into book form. She has been very patient with me as to time invested and understanding of some of the processes of book writing. She is a great woman of faith who wants to lift the Lord up in any way she can.

Last, but not least, we'd both like to thank Shelly Beck for the graphic design work she did on the cover. Her artistic abilities added the final touch to this project.

Introduction

Anyone who is seeking to live a committed Christian life is involved in all-out spiritual warfare. In this life, it is absolutely necessary to stand by our convictions. But how does a committed believer battle life's pressures? There is a constant barrage of isolation, indoctrination, pressure to compromise, and confusion. How do we handle these?

Much of the book of Daniel reminds us about the spiritual warfare that underlies human history. And it is a story about a man who lived an exemplary life in the midst of this warfare. For 73 years, between the ages of 17 - 90, Daniel had been under constant pressure from a pagan society in which he was forced to live day in and day out. When faced with the pressures of living in that society, Daniel always stood firm in his convictions and continued to live his life based on commitment to God.

As we take a look at the first six chapters of the book of Daniel, we are challenged by the life of Daniel to take a stand for our Lord in our own day and in our own daily situations, even when being the only one standing is not easy or comfortable.

Chapter 1

Standing By Our Convictions
Daniel 1:1-21

Anyone who is seeking to live a committed Christian life, whether they believe it or not or whether they understand it or not, is involved in all-out spiritual warfare. Standing by your spiritual convictions is absolutely necessary!

Pastor Andy Stanley tells about his first date with his wife, Sandy. He said that after the first five minutes he ran out of things to say and was grasping for straws. He turned to her and used this line (it's a great line) "Sandy, do you ever do any modeling?" (I mean he's got her believing he thinks she is beautiful enough to be a model – great first impression, huh?) She answered, "Well, I used to." He could tell by the tone of her voice that this was a touchy subject, but being more inquisitive than sensitive, he went on, "Tell me about it."

She told him this story. When she first went to Georgia Tech as a student, she got some opportunities to do some modeling. That was good because she made some extra money to help pay for school. Then she got an invitation to model for a costume company. She and three other girls were to model costumes for people choosing outfits for an upcoming costume party.

When she got to the dressing room, Sandy found that each person was to model four costumes. Sandy went out on the runway in the first costume and came back. In the dressing room Sandy looked at the second costume she was to model and decided, "I can't wear that." She looked behind it at the third one which was just as bad. By that time, it was her turn to go out again. Instead, she put on her own clothes and went to tell her employers she couldn't model the other costumes.

"Why?", exclaimed her employer, "We're doing a show. I'm paying you. You will ruin the show." Sandy replied, "I'm sorry. I don't expect to be paid for this, and I understand I've made things difficult for you." The other girls looked at her as if to say, "You're just modeling. This isn't a statement about your morality." Sandy said, "I'm sorry. I can't model this. I'm through."

That was the end of her modeling career. Andy Stanley said "When she told me that, my estimation of her and the way I valued her as a person went sky high because I'd found a woman who cared more about what God thought than what the world thought. I knew that's the kind of woman I wanted to marry. And that's the kind of man I want to be." (Preaching Today, Tape #98)

To care more about what God thinks than what your boyfriend or girlfriend thinks, to care more about what God thinks than what your peers think, to care more about what God thinks than what your employer thinks! That is conviction!

Anyone who is seeking to live a committed Christian Life, whether they believe it or not or whether they understand it or not, is involved in all-out spiritual warfare. We see in Daniel 1:1-2 that Daniel and his friends were taken captive from Jerusalem, God's Holy City, to Babylon, a heathen city that was very hostile to God and godly things. Many Bible scholars believe Daniel was the ripe old age of 17 when he was taken captive along with a number of other teenagers of royal and noble blood. They were conscripted by Nebuchadnezzar, king of Babylon, to serve in his palace.

Their challenge was: How do you live and work in a heathen setting that is not friendly and maybe even hostile to godly things and still not compromise your religious convictions? Does this sound like your dilemma at your job or at school? This is the situation many, many believers are in today. It's right where most of you are living today.

The spiritual warfare in this area takes many forms that challenge our spiritual convictions. On the surface it looked like a real break and an opportunity for genuine promotion for Daniel. All the young men who were conscripted for palace service were going to be given a scholarship that covered tuition and board at the prestigious Babylon University. Sounds so great on the surface, but there was a spiritual price to be paid if they went along with it without taking a stand. Look at the description of the three-year course they were to take at good old BU. Here we see spiritual warfare at work.

At Babylon University there would be a real possibility of isolation from spiritual things – true worship of the holy God and fellowship with believers in God would not be convenient and would take real discipline and effort.

At good old BU there would certainly be an attempt at indoctrination in heathen ways and thinking. Daniel 1:4 says "He was to teach them the language and literature of the Babylonians." The course was designed to change their thinking. Let there be no doubt about it, both the language and especially the literature of the Babylonians was riddled with heathenistic ideas and teachings. These things could easily break down resistance to evil and sinful ways and could easily gnaw away at godly convictions.

At BU there would be pressure to compromise, v. 5, "The king assigned them a daily amount of food and wine from the kings table." – this was designed to change their lifestyle. The main problem here was that besides being unhealthy, this diet was made up of food that had been sacrificed and offered to the heathen gods of Babylon. Daniel and his companions were not to have anything to do with heathen gods and to eat this food, to them, was the same as abandoning their holy, one and only true God for idols and pagan gods. Also, this strategy in this spiritual warfare included confusion, v. 7, "The chief official (who was also Head Master of BU) gave them new names: to Daniel, the name of Belteshazzar; to Hananaih, Saddrach; to Mishael, Meschach; and to Azariah, Abednago." – what's going on here?

To put it very simply, these young men were given their names so they would always keep their minds focused on God – Daniel includes the name of God, Hananiah includes the name of the Lord, Mishael includes the name of God, and Azariah includes the name of the Lord. The new names given to them – Belteshazzar, Shadrach, Meschach, and Abednego were all names that included the names of Babylon's pagan gods: Bel, Nego, and others.

This renaming process could have eaten away at these young men's real identity and purpose in life. These men belonged to God and were born to serve the One, True, Living God and there could be no confusion in their minds and hearts about their real identity or purpose in life. You need to notice that Daniel is never referred to as Belteshazzar in the rest of the book. There was no hint of confusion about who Daniel belonged to – he belonged to the God of the universe.

Solomon tells us there is nothing new under the sun and that is true when it comes to spiritual warfare. It may seem new to us but Satan uses the same methods today as he did even back in the days of these young men. Satan's use of isolation on believers today is rampant in the church. He works very, very hard to get struggling believers to stay away from church and fellow supporting believers. The glow of one piece of coal when it is separated from the bed of coals will quickly die and go out, but keep it in the bed of coals and it will keep burning brightly. Even so, a believer that is isolated from fellow believers will quickly die spiritually; but if they stay in fellowship with other believers, they can keep the fire burning.

The powers of hell are in an all-out press to indoctrinate believers today. Television, computers, godless news reporters, Hollywood, and music are all a part of this indoctrination process. We need to be very discerning about what we see and hear and believe today. The pressure to compromise is all around us pushing, shoving, egging us on. "Everybody's doing it. It's such a little thing. You won't get a promotion if you don't go along with it. You will look intolerant." "Hey, just give me $900 for the car and I will sign a statement for the Department of Motor Vehicles that you only paid me $500 and it will save you money. Nobody will know." Standing by your convictions may cost you money or influence or position, but you are better off losing those things than you are losing your integrity by compromise. Remember, Satan is the master of confusion. He is continually bombarding God's people with confusion that leaves us off balance and easy prey to Satan's thrust and darts. It's hard to think straight, to sort things out, to make what seems like wise decisions. You've been there and you have been tempted to give into that.

> *Anyone who is seeking to live a committed Christian life, whether they believe it or not or whether they understand it or not, is involved in all-out spiritual warfare.*

Battling Life's Pressures
Daniel 1:8-21

How does a committed believer battle this constant barrage of isolation, indoctrination, pressure to compromise, and confusion? Daniel and his teen friends give a wonderful model for the servant of God as we are engaged in spiritual warfare.

Daniel was decisive, v. 8, "But Daniel resolved not to defile himself with the royal food and wine, ..." Decisiveness was critical! Satan and his forces just poured it on Daniel and his friends with isolation, indoctrination, pressure to compromise, and with confusion, "But..." Something between his Lord and Daniel had already taken place before all this pressure came upon him. Before this all came up, Daniel had already made a resolve about things that would defile his relationship to his God. Present behavior cannot be explained apart from past faithfulness or faithlessness. Daniel had already determined beforehand under God's direction and guidance how he would respond to anything that would defile him. He had made a total commitment of himself and he wasn't going to let that slip no matter what tempted him.

Daniel was tactful under the guidance of the Holy Spirit. He used the inner strength God had given him humbly and with respect. He picked the right time and used the right approach to express his concern to the Head Master of BU. Daniel waited until the Head Master was alone so he wouldn't be pressured by the opinions of others and did everything he could not to embarrass his superior. Daniel didn't use harsh words, but asked permission, v. 8, "...he asked the chief official for permission not to defile himself this way." He had prepared suggestions on how to work it out so it would not cause the chief official any problems at all. Daniel did not flaunt his religion, or brag, or show any pride. He only wanted to glorify God in his life.

And Daniel trusted God to help him take a stand. Daniel believed God would be faithful if he was faithful. He knew God could act on his behalf and he trusted God to act on his behalf if he took a stand for God. Was he right in trusting God in this? Even as Daniel was working on the challenge, we see God was working. Daniel didn't know that for sure, but it happened, v. 9, "Now God had caused the official to show favor and sympathy to Daniel..."; v. 15, "...they looked healthier and better nourished than any of the young men who ate the royal food."; v. 17, "To these four young men God gave knowledge and understanding of all kinds of literature and learning. And Daniel could understand visions and dreams of all kinds." As Satan and the evil system tried to indoctrinate these young men, God gave them "knowledge and understanding" that helped them see through the indoctrination and to see how to use this stuff to honor and glorify God. Because of God's help in their lives we see in v. 20 that this heathen king saw these young men were "ten times better" than all their worldly competition. Isn't that just like our Lord!

Growth in grace and usefulness of service does not begin in a world of dreams but in the context of life's harsh realities. How we need decisiveness today! You need to decide once and for all what is God's will for you in the area of physical and moral purity. Make up your mind before you get in the back seat of a car with a guy or a gal or before you get into an apartment or house alone with the other person. Be decisive – "I will go absolutely no farther than this, no matter what or no matter who until I am married to my partner for life." Be decisive – have it settled in your mind and heart what godly honesty is before you get into the workplace where a neat item can be laying for the taking – "I cannot do this no matter what because this is dishonest."

We need to be totally dependent upon the Lord for strength so we can be tactful under the direction of the Holy Spirit when it comes to standing by our convictions. False pride, arrogance, and harshness, even for godly causes, will not bring influence and respect in a touchy situation. And how we need to trust God when it comes to standing up for our convictions. You be faithful to God and God will be faithful to you. He will work along with you as you work with Him. Living for God's glory produces a spirit of humble confidence that God will act on our behalf.

> *God is looking for faithful men and women whom he can elevate to positions of influence.*

Life Application

You who go by the name of Christian, how long has it been since you took a stand based upon that name? When have you last asked what Christ would do or where He would take a stand? What would Jesus do? Have you made up your mind about moral and ethical issues that are grey areas? In any area of life, have you made up your mind that regardless of the consequences, you will not compromise? God is not looking for influential people he can make faithful. God is looking for faithful men and women, whom He can elevate to positions of influence.

You see, we are tempted to think that God is looking for athletes, rock stars, television stars, and wealthy people to make into Christians so He can have influential people of faith. The first chapter of Daniel shows us that the opposite is true. God was looking for some committed teens to be faithful to Him no matter what and when they showed they were faithful He began to raise them to positions of influence, v. 21, "And Daniel remained there (in Babylonia, Satan's citadel) until the first year of King Cyrus." Daniel was a man of tremendous influence for God and Godliness for 70 years and in three world empires and five dynasties.

By God's help, be decisive and tactfully take a stand for Him and His cause when you must! He will bless you for it.

NOTES

Chapter 2

God is the Answer
Daniel 2:1-7; 17-23; 46-49

Sometimes in this "taking a stand for the Lord" business it seems like it's "out of the frying pan and into the fire. I mean, in chapter one, we find Daniel courageously taking a stand for his Lord and coming through a very tense situation with flying colors. As a 17-year-old teenager we read that "Daniel resolved not to defile himself" and that resolve was in direct conflict with King Nebuchadnezzar's plan and mode of operation. Daniel took a stand and God blessed him for his faithfulness in wonderful ways. It looked like Daniel and his friends were going to live happy ever after even though they were captives in a pagan country.

And then it happened.

"Knock, Knock."

"Who's there?"

Arioch, the commander of the king's guards."

Arioch, the commander of the king's guards who?"

Arioch, the commander of the king's guards who is going to execute you because of the king's command!"

Can you imagine Daniel's reaction? "You've got to be kidding! The king was so happy with my friends and me. What happened?" Arioch, who seemed to be well acquainted with Daniel and seemed to have much trust in him, gives Daniel this information.

- Old King Neb had a dream that left him deeply troubled – might have eaten dill pickle ice cream.

- He didn't have any idea what the dream meant; in fact he didn't even know what the dream was!

- It appears the King was getting sick and tired of his fawning advisors – the magicians, enchanters, sorcerers, and astrologers. They were a bunch of "yes-men" who didn't have any answers at all.

- The King called a meeting and told them they were really like his cabinet, that he was deeply troubled by this dream; and they told him if he would tell them the dream, they could "concoct," – no they were sure they could interpret this troubling dream.

- It was then old King Neb lowered the boom on the whole bunch of them:

  "This is what I have firmly decided: If you do not tell me what the dream was and interpret it, I will have you cut into pieces and your houses turned into piles of rubble" (v.5).

- The king's cabinet howls, "Unfair! Unfair!"

- The cabinet also said something worthwhile for once, "What the kings asks is too difficult. No one can reveal it to the king except the gods" (vs. 11). They were right there, for only God can know what people truly think in their subconscious. They go on, "…and they do not live among men." They got that wrong, for we have already seen that the One True God does live among men – men like Daniel and his friends who love Him and seek to be true to Him.

The clock for King Neb's cabinet and Daniel and his friends, who somehow got lumped in with these guys, was ticking and they had no answer or didn't know where to go for the answer. But Daniel knew where to go for the answer because Daniel knew that God is the answer to so many of life's problems and challenges. You've seen the bumper sticker, "Jesus is the Answer!" and many of you have also seen another bumper sticker, "What's the Question?" Those poor folks who mock the declaration "Jesus is the Answer!" have never come to the confidence in the Lord that Daniel had.

> *Daniel knew where to go for the answer because Daniel knew that God is the answer to so many of life's problems and challenges.*

God is the Answer To Life's Problems
Daniel 2:1-23

God is the answer to many of life's problems and challenges. The question is: "What do you do when you are doing your best to take a stand for God and the heat is turned up?" In Daniel 2:11-23, we see how Daniel handled that question. He went to the King knowing that God was indeed the answer. Notice that Daniel was not flippant about his knowledge of God's ability to give answers, nor was he brash. In verse 14, Daniel spoke to the king's officer "with wisdom and tact." Then Daniel went to the king and "asked for time so that he might interpret the dream for him." (v. 16). Daniel had confidence that "God is the Answer", so he could believe that by God's help he could interpret the king's dream.

Next, Daniel "urged" his Jewish friends to "plead for mercy from the God of heaven concerning this mystery…" (vs. 18); He wanted them to go to God in earnest prayer. They prayed remembering, "God is the Answer". I'm sure they had a very intense and urgent prayer meeting over this request, partly because this included a prayer that they "might not be executed with the rest of the wise men of Babylon." (v. 18). As they prayed, God gave the answer. "During the night the mystery was revealed to Daniel in a vision." (v. 19). When we really, truly know "God is the Answer", we pray differently.

Then Daniel praised God for the answer to his prayers (vv. 19-23). This praise was not just for saving their Jewish hides. This praise was for what was revealed to Daniel through the answer to prayer. God has all the wisdom and power needed. Daniel knew that it is God who sets up kings and deposes them. It is God who gives wisdom to the wise and knowledge to the discerning. It is God who reveals deep and hidden things (vs. 21). Daniel also praised God for making known to him, personally, what he asked for: what the king's dream was and the interpretation of that dream. God forgive us for how often we don't remember to give thanks and praise to our Lord for answers to prayer. Daniel took absolutely no credit for what had happened. He gave all glory and praise to God. You can't speak for God until you've spent some time with God.

> *When we really, truly know "God is the answer," we pray differently.*

God is the Answer to Human History
Daniel 2:24-49

The question here is "What is the world coming to?" The answer God gives concerning human history could never be discovered by human wisdom. Many people do not know that Daniel contains the ABC's of prophecy – it is the primer of biblical prophecy in so many ways. So many people get all excited about studying the Book of Revelation because they are so intrigued with all the prophecy found there; but studying Revelation without studying Daniel is certainly frustrating and probably useless. You cannot understand the Book of Revelation until you have some basic understanding of the Book of Daniel. Human history is about "changing times and seasons," about "setting up kings and deposing them," about "deep and hidden things" which is what Daniel praised the Lord for revealing to him in vv. 20-23.

What is the world coming to? Check out King Neb's dream and the interpretation of that dream that God gave to Daniel. Here the divine message emphasizes that the key to understanding the rise and fall of empires and emperors is not military or financial, but rather moral and spiritual.

In his dream, the king saw a "dazzling statue, awesome in appearance" (v. 31). The king's dream had a lot to do with "setting up kings and deposing them." We see in vv. 36-38 that the head of gold represented the Babylonian Empire, which King Nebuchadnezzar headed. Daniel was pretty straightforward about that. In v. 39 we see that the chest and arms of the statue were of silver and they represented an inferior kingdom, the Medo-Persian Empire (Daniel 8:20 identifies this empire). The belly and thighs of the statue were of bronze and represented the Grecian Empire

27

(Daniel 8:21 identifies this empire). The legs of the statue were of iron and the feet were of iron mixed with clay (v. 40) and represented the Roman Empire.

In this revelation we're talking hundreds of years before the Roman Empire would appear. After this fourth empire comes into power, there appears a "rock" (v. 34), which crushes the statue, the world empires, and becomes a mountain that fills the whole earth, and this Kingdom will never end. Notice that Daniel tells King Neb that no wise man, enchanter, magician or diviner can explain to the king the mystery he has asked about, but "there is a God in heaven who reveals mysteries..." (v. 27). It is the great God that "has shown the king what will take place in the future. The dream is true and the interpretation is trust-worthy." (v. 45).

The question now is: What is this mighty, heathen despot named King Nebuchadnezzar doing down on his face on the floor? The answer is: He realizes God is truly "The Answer". From King Neb's own mouth come these words, "Surely your God is the God of gods and the Lord of kings and a revealer of mysteries, for you were able to reveal the mystery." (v.47). The king was awed, but not converted. Though he didn't reject his pagan gods, he at least acknowledged that Daniel's God was more powerful than any "god" he had ever worshipped.

Life Application

Was it worth standing up for right in this very tense, life-threatening situation? Daniel and his friends would have said, "Absolutely yes!" Verse 48 tells us that King Nebuchadnezzar made Daniel ruler over the "entire province of Babylon and placed him in charge of its wise men." As ruler, Daniel appointed his friends over the province of Babylon. If you truly believe "God is the Answer" to life's problems and challenges, you will find it so much easier to take a stand for God.

Life will be full of challenges and there might be times in this "Taking a Stand for God" business when you will feel like you are going out of the frying pan and into the fire. But let me assure you, when you take a stand for God, you are taking a stand upon the Rock of Nebuchadnezzar's vision; you are taking a stand for Jesus Christ the Lord. His Kingdom will fill the whole earth and His kingdom will never end. As John writes in the Book of Revelation, 11:15, "The kingdom of the world has become the kingdom of our Lord and of his Christ, and He will reign for ever and ever."

This Rock, this Stone, is the "Stone the builders rejected (it) has become the capstone…a stone that causes men to stumble and a rock that makes them fall." (1 Peter 2:7-8). King Jesus is King of kings and Lord of lords. Hallelujah! Bow down before him in humility and with adoration and praise. Then determine by His help that you will take a stand for Him.

NOTES

Chapter 3

Trial By Fire
Daniel 3:1-30

These first six chapters of Daniel have been challenging us about the matter of taking a stand for our Lord in our day and in our daily situations. Being the only one standing is not easy or comfortable.

A man was visiting a church in another city and a particular hymn was announced at the start of the service. When they sang that particular hymn at his home church they ALWAYS stood. As the introduction to the hymn was being played, the man jumped to his feet. The rest of the congregation began to sing the song and he was standing there, all by his lonesome, looking around and seeing that no one else in the entire church was standing. He slithered down in his seat trying to look as small and inconspicuous as possible (ODB 4-6-92)

You can imagine how embarrassing it was to be the only one standing – even in that rather harmless situation. When you take a stand, all eyes are on you. You have lost a convenient place to disappear into the crowd and you have put yourself on the line.

As we move through these chapters, we begin to wonder who is really on trial here. Daniel and his friends are hundreds of miles from home. They are surrounded by people speaking a language foreign to them. They have nothing to look back on but a temple (now in rubble) and a homeland (now in enemy hands). Surely God is dead – or at least asleep- to have so forgotten His exalted people, right? Not if you ask Daniel and his three friends! For them, God is still very much alive; answering prayer, interpreting dreams, honoring the integrity of those committed to Him.

So who really is on trial here? In chapter one we saw *heathen customs* being judged by God Almighty: the customs of eating food sacrificed to idols and giving deference to heathen gods. In chapter two we saw *heathen philosophy* being judged: Heathen philosophy called for predicting the future by checking the stars and secret charms. Now we will look at how *heathen pride* is being judged. Nebuchadnezzar, the loose cannon emperor of the first world empire, thought he was the greatest; greater than the One, true God.

> *Real courage is fear that has said its prayers.*

EVERYBODY is Doing It!
Daniel 3:1-12

This chapter begins with a huge mass of people, thousands of them Babylonian officials, down on their faces on the sands of the Plains of Dura before a stupid idol made by King Nebuchadnezzar. You see, King Neb didn't like God's verdict about what the world, and his kingdom, were coming to. You remember in chapter 2 that the verdict of the one, true God was that the Babylonian Empire was the Head of Gold in Neb's dream. That was pretty good with Neb being the first Emperor. But chapter 3 is a study in forgotten lessons. After the wonderful revelations of chapter 2, Neb had humbled himself before God and recognized Him as "the God of gods and the Lord of kings and a revealer of mysteries." (Daniel 2:47). But Neb could not be contented with his empire being just the Head of Gold on the statue. He made a statue of ALL gold – gold plated that is. He would not settle for just a head of gold, but wanted his empire to be the whole thing. Instead of gratitude, it was rebellion. Instead of honoring God, it was self-deification.

That statue must have been pretty impressive, set on a huge mound of earth on the plain of Dura with a height of 90 feet and a width of 9 feet. All the Babylonian officials were brought to the base of the statue and the people were told to "bow or burn". The golden statue was gleaming in the afternoon sun; the music of the Babylonian Symphony sounded with "bowing music"; and everybody fell with their foreheads in the dust before King Neb's statue. The truth was that EVERYBODY was doing it. Everyone except our three young Jewish friends of chapter 1: Shadrach, Meshach, and Abednego.

There were other officials in the Babylonian Empire who just couldn't accept that these Jewish young men had been promoted ahead of them. Out of the thousands upon thousands of people bowing before King Neb's statue, there were just three who did not bow. Their enemies were just watching for a chance to get them in trouble with the Emperor and they "hot-footed it" to the king to tell him what he already knew, "They neither serve your gods, nor worship the image of gold you have set up…" (v. 12).

We hear it said constantly today, "Everybody's doing it!" As if that is the only justification we need for doing stupid, sinful, goofy things. If you think you can stand before God in eternity and tell Him, "Well, everybody was doing it" and He will accept that for an excuse for compromising in sinful, grey areas; boy have you got a surprise coming. Some argue in tough situations like this: "Can't you bow your knees, but stand up in your head?" They're kind of like the little boy who was being punished for being naughty and time out involved sitting down in a corner of the room. The little boy sassily replied to his mother when she put him in the chair, "I might be *sitting down* on the outside, but I'm *standin' up* on the inside!" That doesn't work with Mom and it certainly doesn't work with God. How often we use the excuse that everybody is doing it as a cover for our soft, anemic, spiritual backbone. There's no taking a stand there.

The Lines Are Drawn
Daniel 3:13-18

In this taking a stand for God business, there comes a time when all the wisdom and tact in the world will no longer work in relating to evil people. In verses 13-18 of chapter 3, the lines were clearly drawn. Chapters 1 and 2 emphasized how Daniel used humility and tact as he took a stand. But in chapter 3 the issues were too clear and what the king was trying to do was too blatantly wrong for any measure of compromise. The kings said, "Bow or burn."

These three young men knew the commandments of their God, which included "You shall have no other gods before me." and "You shall not make idols or bow down to them." The bottom line was: these young men's reverential fear of God was greater than their fear of the great Emperor Nebuchadnezzar of Babylon. It is so true that "real courage is fear that has said its prayers."

True faith is not linked to circumstances or consequences. It is founded upon the unchanging faithfulness of God. The king proposed a second chance for them, but there comes a time when all the wisdom and tact in the world will no longer be of any use when dealing with evil people. Their response to the second chance was, "Nebuchadnezzar, we do not need to defend ourselves before you in this matter. If we are thrown into the blazing furnace, the God we serve is able to save us from it, and he will rescue us from your hand, O king. But even if he does not, we will not serve your gods or worship the image made of gold you have set up." (Daniel 3:16-18). You talk about taking a stand! There are no "ifs, ands, or buts" about where these young men stood on the issue. If we truly have reverential fear for our Lord, we will be far more concerned about honoring God than honoring men.

When a doctor performs surgery, the attending nurse must keep careful tab of the number of hemostats and sponges used so that an incision is not closed until each item has been removed and accounted for. A young nurse on her first day with this duty told the surgeon he had used 12 sponges, but she could only account for 11. The doctor curtly announced that he had removed them all. The young nurse insisted that one was missing, but the doctor grimly declared he would proceed with the suturing. The nurse, her eyes blazing, said, "You can't do that! Think of the patient!" The doctor smiled and, lifting his foot, showed the nurse the 12th sponge, which he had deliberately dropped on the floor. "You'll do!" he said. He'd been testing her to see if she had the courage and integrity to carry out the duties of her position. When will we come to the place where we are willing to say, "You can't do that! I can't do that! What about God?" When you care more about what God thinks and what God feels than what your peers think or feel, that is conviction and that is the place from which we can take a stand. (OBD 5-23-69)

> *When you care more about what God thinks than what your peers think, that is conviction!*

Trial By Fire
Daniel 3:19-30

You can count on it: taking a stand may cause you to go through a trial by fire (vv 19-30). Peter reminds us, "Dear friends, do not be surprised at the painful trial you are suffering, as though something strange were happening to you…" (1 Peter 4:12).

Shadrach, Meshach, and Abednego had already counted the cost. They were bound (probably tied hand and foot) and thrown into the fire that was so hot that those who threw them in were killed by the intense heat. The Scripture narration seems to indicate that the moment they were in the fire, the king "leaped to his feet in amazement" (v. 24). He did a head count. He had 3 young men thrown into the fire and the fire had not touched them, except to burn off their bonds from their arms and feet. Sometimes it is in the trial by fire that we finally lose the bondage that has dogged us for a long period of time. When we submit to our Lord so completely that we are willing to face the trial by fire for His namesake, it is then we become free from some of the bondage in our lives. Now, instead of three young men in the fire, the king saw four. The fourth one "looks like a son of the gods." (v. 25). The Lord Jesus Christ was in the midst of the trial with them. Isaiah speaks for God' in Isaiah 43:2-3 and tells God's people, "When you pass through the waters, I will be with you; and when you pass through the rivers they will not sweep over you. When you walk through the fire, you will not be burned; the flames will not set you ablaze. For I am the Lord your God, the Holy One of Israel, your Savior."

The Rock of chapter 2 that would destroy all earthly kingdoms and fill the earth with His presence was in their fiery trial. The Lord never promised to keep us *from* the fire, but he did promise to always be with us *in* the fire. Those young Hebrew men came out of the fire and the divine record says, "They saw that the fire had not harmed their bodies, nor was a hair of their heads singed; their robes were not scorched, and there was no smell of fire on them." (v. 27).

Once again, King Neb is praising the one, true God and his servants, Shadrach, Meshach, and Abednego for trusting in God and even for defying his stupid command. He notes that they "…were willing to give up their lives rather than serve or worship any god except their own God." (v. 28). The good king demanded that everyone in the empire show due respect to this God "for no other god can save in this way." (v. 29) and once more these young men are promoted in the kingdom.

Our trial by fire may not land us in a furnace, but it may make us very uncomfortable, even desperate. The essence of faith is the willingness to serve God without a guarantee. Many stories of heroism don't end positively. A missionary is captured by rebels and in spite of many prayers is murdered. Dietrich Bonhoeffer defied the Nazis in the name of God, but a few days before the war ended, he was executed. Why wasn't God in the furnace then? The truth is, He was in their furnace, too. We marvel at the Hebrews 11 account of those who took a stand and went through trial by fire and came through with flying colors: 33 people "who through faith conquered kingdoms, administered justice, and gained what was promised, who shut the mouth of lions, quenched the fury of the flames and escaped the edge of the sword… women received back their dead, raised to life again." But we are taken aback by v. 35b, "Others were tortured and refused to be released so that they might gain a better resurrection. Some faced jeers and flogging, while still others were chained and put in prison.

They were stoned; they were sawed in two; they were put to death by the sword." It sounds like something went wrong in the middle of v. 35, but that could not be further from the truth for we read, "These were all commended for their faith, yet none of them received what had been promised. God had planned something better for us..."

The question is this: "When all you have left is your confidence in God, is that enough?" Daniel's friends found that with nothing to cling to but God, God was all they needed. One fellow who had been going through a terrible trial by fire testified, "I never knew Jesus Christ was all I needed until Jesus Christ was all I had."

> *I never knew Jesus was all
> I needed until Jesus Christ
> was all I had.*

Life Application

Remembering Daniel is a prophetic book, we need to look at Revelation 13:14-15 at the end of this message. Remembering Neb's golden statue and what he tried to do with it, listen to these words from the book of Revelation, "He (the demonic beasts of the end time) ordered them to set up an image in honor of the beast who was wounded by the sword and yet lived. He was given power to give breath to the image of the first beast, so that it could speak and cause all who refused to worship the image to be killed."

Maybe your trials by fire are just inconveniences today, but there is coming a day when many, many will go through much the same that Daniel's friends did. And you and I might still have to face a trial by fire in our lives in the near future. Are you committed to staying true to God no matter the cost?

Do those in your world know that you have taken a firm stand on the side of God and truth? Or are you a spineless, timid, wavering Christian? When Constantius, the father of Constantine (Constantine was the emperor of the Roman Empire who turned the empire to Christianity) came to the throne, there were many Christians in public office. He proceeded to issue an edict requiring all Christians to forsake their faith or give up their places of trust in his realm. Most of them immediately gave up their employment in order to preserve a good conscience, but a few cringed and renounced Christianity. When the emperor had thus tested them, he dismissed everyone who had complied with his stern order and took all the Christians back again. He accounted for his strange conduct by saying, "It is my firm belief that those who would not be true to Christ would not be true to me!" (ODB

3-33-71). How the saints rejoiced, for not only had they brought honor to the Lord by their actions, but they also had gained stature in the eyes of Constantius.

When faithfulness is the most difficult it is then the most necessary! Will our Lord find us faithful in taking a stand for him even if it means going through trial by fire?

> *When faithfulness is the most difficult, it is then the most necessary!*

NOTES

Chapter 4

Telling It Like It Is
Daniel 4: 1-37

It was now testimony time. Suppose I told you that Saddam Hussein posted a story on the Internet in which he related a very personal experience. For seven years he lost his mind and lived in the Middle Eastern desert subsisting on wild plants and grass. At night he slept in the open air and in the evening his body was drenched with dew. His shaggy hair grew until it reached his waist and his finger-nails looked like eagles' claws. In essence, he lived like an animal, unable to think or reason like a human being.

Then one day, Hussein came to his senses. His mind was restored. He bathed, clothed himself, cut his hair, and trimmed his nails. He then returned to Baghdad and once again became king of Iraq. However, he was a different man now. He acknowledged for the whole world to hear that the "gods" he had worshiped – power, sensuality and money – were all false and a reflection of his own arrogance. He explained that his view of Allah was a distorted and false view of deity. He proclaimed that he now worshiped the one true God – the God of the Bible, the God of his own father Abraham. His final words were gripping. He admitted his pride and proclaimed: "Now I, Saddam Hussein, praise and exalt and glorify the King of heaven, because everything He does is right and all his ways are just. And those who walk in pride He is able to humble (adapted from Daniel 4:37).

Obviously this story is not true. It would be exciting if it were. However, this is exactly what happened to Nebuchadnezzar, the king of Babylon – the man who Saddam Hussein declares is his hero. The territory of modern Iraq is a part of the area King Nebuchadnezzar ruled over. In Daniel 4 we see that the Lord humbled King Nebuchadnezzar who was the first world emperor and a royal ruler.

As Nebuchadnezzar introduces this chapter, he tells us about "the miraculous signs and wonders that the Most High God has performed for me." (v 2). These signs and wonders really got Neb's attention and made a true believer out of him. He became convinced that "His (God's) kingdom is an eternal kingdom; his dominion endures from generation to generation." (v. 3).

In the past God had done some pretty amazing things to convince, nay, convert, King Neb; but Neb didn't quite get it. On two previous occasions in chapters 2 and 3 Nebuchadnezzar's heart had been stirred to consider spiritual realities; but each time he fell back into spiritual lethargy. Through the powerful workings of God and God's servant, Daniel, "telling it like it is" King Neb was dramatically converted to a true believer in God.

Wake Up Call
Daniel 4:4-18

We see in vv 4-18 that the conversion of King Nebuchadnezzar began with a wake up call in the form of a terrifying
dream. The wake up call came in verse 4 when Neb was
feeling very contented and prosperous. He had conquered
nation after nation. He had brought all the various peoples
of those nations into his world-wide empire. Finally, he
was firmly in control. Things were going very well for
King Neb – it couldn't have been going better. Then he
had this dream that left him "afraid" and "terrified" (v. 5).

Again he calls his cabinet - the magicians, enchanters,
astrologers, and diviners. When would he ever learn?
They could not interpret the dream even though he
described it to them. Even if they could have interpreted it,
it was unlikely that they'd tell the king the real meaning of
the dream, fearing for their own lives. He finally calls for
Daniel, whom he knew had the Spirit of God in him.

King Nebuchadnezzar described the terrifying dream to
Daniel in great detail; and, when Daniel comprehends what
the dream means, we read that "his thoughts terrified him."
(v. 19). So now we have two leaders who are in real
anguish over a dream that the Lord has given to King Neb.
Neb is terrified about what it could mean to him and his
world empire. Daniel is terrified about what it could mean
to him if he interprets it as he knows God wants him to.

We are all inclined to dream our way through life until
someone or something confronts us with the "real world".
A new recruit was rudely awakened by his platoon sergeant

after his first night in an army barracks. "It's four-thirty!" bellowed the sergeant – what a wake up call. "Four-thirty!" gasped the rookie. "Man, you'd better go to bed. We have a big day ahead of us tomorrow!" (ODB, 1/9/92). Cancer, heart-attack – God will not spare our bodies if that is what it takes to save our souls. "Your job is through today. Clean your desk out and leave." What will it take to wake us up?

> *God will not spare our bodies if that is what it takes to save our souls.*

Daniel 'Tells It Like It Is'
Daniel 4:19-27

Here we see that Daniel needs to take a stand. It is time for
him to 'tell it like it is'. To take a stand and 'tell it like it
is' could have been very costly for Daniel. Remember,
Neb was well known for his short fuse temper. He had a
reputation for being very unstable. This is the king who got
so mad that he had Shadrach, Meshach, and Abednego
thrown into a furnace that he had heated seven times hotter
because he was so angry. This is the king who had said
that if things didn't go his way that he would cut those
involved into pieces and turn their houses into piles of
rubble Daniel 2:5). This is the same king of whom a top
government official told Daniel that if things did not go the
way the king wanted them to, he would have his head
(Daniel 1:10).

Now Daniel has to tell King Neb that God's judgment was
going to come on him in a very, very devastating way.
Daniel knows that he must obey God rather than men and
so he proceeds to tell the king the truth. Before he does,
however, he tells the king that he wished this prophecy
applied to the king's enemies instead of him (v 19). But
Daniel must let the king know the true interpretation of the
dream. Neb had dreamed of an enormous tree that was
visible to the ends of the earth, even as King Neb's empire
was an enormous empire that was very visible to the ends
of the earth. The tree was beautiful and abundant in fruit
and the inhabitants of the earth were sheltered and fed by
this amazing tree. God's word was that Neb and his empire
was in fact that enormous tree.

Then there was this "holy messenger" in the dream that had
this message concerning the tree, "Cut it down. Strip the

47

leaves and scatter its fruit." In the midst of his pride and prosperity, old King Neb was going to be cut down and his influence was going to be stripped from him. He was to live like an animal until seven times, (or seven years) would pass. This would go on, Daniel had to tell King Neb, "…until you acknowledge that the Most High is sovereign over the kingdoms of men and gives them to anyone He wishes." (v. 25). Then his kingdom would be given back to him and God would prosper him once more.

When Daniel had taken his stand and did 'tell it like it is', he then gave the emperor some advice in verse 27. The advice is very straightforward: "Renounce your sins by doing what is right and your wickedness by being kind to the oppressed." Daniel then adds these words of wisdom and hope, "It may be that then your prosperity will continue." Daniel was as honest and straightforward as he could possibly be. He was true to His Lord and the emperor by telling the truth no matter what the cost was going to be to him personally. He took a stand for His Lord under the most trying circumstances.

Will you take a stand by 'telling it like it is' if you are called on to? I'm not talking about being obnoxious or abusing people with the truth. But there comes a time when you have to tell the truth no matter the cost. You have to be willing to confront others with the truth.

> *There comes a time when you have to tell the truth no matter the cost.*

Pride Goes Before Destructions
Dan. 4:28-36

In spite of Daniel's and God's faithfulness, they couldn't overcome Neb's foolishness. Just one year from God's revelation of what was going to happen to Neb if he didn't shape up, Neb was inflated to the bursting point with selfish pride. He was now head of the greatest empire the world had ever known up until that time. He had done a number of amazing things – especially with Babylon, the capital city of the empire.

Babylon was surrounded with walls 87 feet thick, 350 feet high and 15 miles long on each side. This was 60 miles of walls for an area of 360 square miles. They could run chariot races on top of those walls with a number of chariots going side by side (I'd want to be in the middle, thank you). The city boasted twenty-five magnificent streets, running in parallel lines north and south, 150 feet wide and 15 miles long, intersected by 25 others of similar dimension running east and west; and a hundred brass gates hung on the walls. There was also the celebrated hanging garden that was one of the seven wonders of the then-known world; and on and on the list of his accomplishments go.

One day the emperor said , "Is not this the great Babylon *I* have built as a royal residence, by *my* mighty power and for the glory of *my* majesty (v. 30). *I, my, my.* Neb had forgotten how much God hates pride as the writer of Proverbs tells us in Proverbs 6:16-19. God can do nothing for us or in us except humble us when we are full of pride.

No sooner had Neb strutted himself about with such pride than the Holy Messenger speaks loud and clear, "This is what is decreed for you, King Nebuchadnezzar: Your royal authority has been taken from you. You will be driven away from people and will live with the wild animals... until you acknowledge that the Most High is sovereign over the kingdoms of men and gives them to anyone he wishes." (vs. 31-32).

The bursting point of Neb's selfish pride collapsed into the abyss of spiritual and mental darkness. That was Neb's lot until one day he "raised his eyes toward heaven," (v. 34). He began to look to God, not self. He began to praise God, and not self. He began to honor and glorify God and not himself. And in the midst of that changing outlook his "sanity was restored" (v.34). Even in his sinful pride, God was faithful to King Nebuchadnezzar.

A person who thinks too much of himself doesn't think enough about God. Pride is the dandelion of the soul. Its roots go deep; only a little left behind sprouts again. Its seeds lodge in the tiniest encouraging cracks and it flourishes in good soil. The danger of pride is that it feeds on goodness. From this chapter we see three key things about pride:

- God hates pride and arrogance (Proverbs 6:16-19)

- Though God hates pride, He is patient and wants us to turn from sin so that He will not have to discipline us.

- God will respond to our prayers for help when we acknowledge our sins and see His help.

Life Application

Thank God for people who take a stand and 'tell it like it is' with as much kindness and care as possible. Where would King Nebuchadnezzar have been without a person like Daniel who was willing to be true to the Lord no matter the cost to him personally. From what we can tell from the fourth chapter of Daniel, it is likely that Nebuchadnezzar is in heaven today. The reason he might be in heaven today is because Daniel stood firm and told him the truth in love.

We worry about the question: "Would a real friend tell..." What would a real friend tell us? They would tell us that our slip is showing, or that we have something hanging out of our nose, or that we have a smudge on our chin. True friends want to save their friends embarrassment and further problems. Would a true friend lovingly and kindly tell a friend that if they don't take some specific steps, they are going to be eternally lost? Will someone say to us some day, "Why didn't you tell me..."

There is no doubt about it. True friends care enough to lovingly and kindly 'tell it like it is'.

True friends care enough to lovingly and kindly "tell it like it is".

NOTES

Chapter 5

Speaking Up for God
Daniel 5:1-31

The book of Daniel reminds us that we are involved in spiritual warfare. As far as "The Kingdoms of this World" vs. "The Kingdom of God" goes, as the book of Daniel begins, it looked like the score was Satan 10 and God 0.

So much of Daniel is about the spiritual warfare that underlies human history. It's hard to see this in the humdrum of life; but we can appreciate this more if we understand the background for the Book of Daniel. God's people had been defeated and God's city, Jerusalem, had been destroyed; and God's nation was firmly under the control of the Babylonian Empire. What makes this so hard to take and to understand is that God let a very wicked Empire defeat God's people, destroy God's city, and possess God's land. Good and faithful Jewish people like Daniel and his friends, Shadrach, Meshach, and Abednego were taken from God's land and subjected to servanthood to pagan Emperors and Empires. The pagan society tried to break them down spiritually, culturally, and emotionally.

But in the book of Daniel the point is being made again and again as John the Revelator tells us in Revelation 11:15, "The kingdom of the world has become the kingdom of our Lord and of His Christ, and He will reign for ever and ever." As the book of Daniel begins, that looks like the farthest thing from the truth. God looked defeated in His own nation and his own city. God's people looked totally defeated as captive servants in a pagan world empire. The kingdoms of this world seemed totally in control. In Daniel the world empires come on the scene of human history with flourish and power. The head of gold, the Babylonian Empire, was so impressive, but today we see it fade from world history. We will see the chest and arms of silver, the Medo-Persian Empire, come on the scene of world history, but we will also see it limp off the stage of world history in Daniel. As the Book of Daniel progresses, we begin to see that God is not defeated. He will settle the score and He, and His Son alone, will reign forever and ever.

We begin to see it happen before our very eyes here in Daniel 5. Thirty years had passed between chapter 4 and chapter 5. King Nebuchadnezzar, the first world Emperor, and Emperor of the Babylonian Empire, had died.

Daniel is now over 80 years old and it appears he had been pretty much forgotten and put on the shelf. There had been a number of assassinations among the children of King Nebuchadnezzar – brother-in-laws murdering brother-in-laws to gain power and prestige – this can all be traced through archaeological findings and the secular history of the Babylonian Empire. Nebuchadnezzar's son-in-law, Nabonidus, was now Emperor of the Babylonian Empire and his son, King Neb's grandson, Belshazzar, is co-ruler with him. But the Medo-Persian Empire had captured all the outposts of the Babylonian Empire and had put the city of Babylon under siege.

It was at this time that the arrogant, young upstart, Belshazzar, decides to do an "in your face God." Daniel 5:23 describes it this way, "You have set yourself up against the Lord of heaven." He thought he was so clearly in control. He gave a banquet for a thousand of his nobles while the city was under siege. He started the banquet with a cocktail party and led the way in promptly getting totally drunk. The banquet quickly became a drunken orgy. At this point he had made a thorough fool of himself and debauched the Empire; but he hadn't crossed the line with God, yet. It was when he got this hair-brained idea of getting the sacred goblets that use to be in God's Temple in Jerusalem and used them to toast the pagan gods of gold, silver, bronze, iron, wood, and stone that he crossed the line. He cloaked his sin as an act of worship. He veiled his blasphemy in the name of religion. That was clearly an "In your face God!" act! Daniel 5:5 tells us that "Suddenly a human hand appeared and wrote on the plaster of the wall." That apparition of doom shocked Belshazzar out of his drunken stupor. He was terrified – "His face turned pale and he was so frightened that his knees knocked together and his legs gave way." (vs. 6). Pandemonium broke loose and it was the Queen Mother, probably Bel's grandmother, who got things back in order. Her strategy was to forget the useless cabinet and call on Daniel who had the Spirit of God ruling in his life.

Belshazzar have been weighed and found to be a spiritual lightweight.

Daniel Speaks Up for God
Daniel 5:13-28

Daniel steps up to the podium. The tables had been turned and it was "In your face, Belshazzar!" It was a morally dark night in Babylon. Darker than your work place, school, or community. King Belshazzar had willfully blasphemed God by desecrating the sacred goblet looted from the temple in Jerusalem. If you look at Daniel's message to Bel, there is no doubt that he was totally responsible for what was happening to him. Listen to the message in verse 28, "<u>You</u> did not honor the God who holds in his hand <u>your</u> life and all life and all <u>your</u> ways." Twelve times in Daniel's message to Bel, He uses the terms "you, your, yourself." Babylon and Belshazzar were about to face God's judgment. Yet in the midst of this gross darkness shone the light of a single witness: the prophet Daniel. Because his reputation as a man with the Spirit of the Holy God, Daniel was summoned to interpret the mystifying message on the wall.

Daniel could have softened God's warning to give it a meaning the king and his court would rather hear. He could have omitted the part about judgment and death. But instead of muddling the message to please the king, Daniel remained true to God. Standing alone before Belshazzar and his drunken court, Daniel boldly spoke the whole truth. He was taking a stand by speaking up for God. It took enormous courage for Daniel to do that; but the threat from an earthly king was nothing compared to his allegiance to the King of Heaven. Daniel feared God so much that he had little fear of Belshazzar.

The message of doom that came to Belshazzar came in the form of four code words that gave a clear message that

Belshazzar understood thoroughly. "Mene, Mene, Tekel, Parsin," (Daniel 5:25). It's kind of like the term Y2K which is a code for "problems and concerns about the year 2000." The first word is repeated twice: Mene, Mene. The code word stood for "Numbered, Numbered".

Tekel was the next code word meaning "Weighed". Parsin was the final code word meaning "Divided". The message was: God is counting down the final moments of your kingdom…10, 9, 8, 7, 6…You have been weighed and found to be a spiritual lightweight. And your kingdom, the once great Babylonian Empire, will be divided among the Medo-Persian Empire. The sad thing is the moment God gave Belshazzar his final call he was drunk – how pathetic! God destroys only those who have known the truth and have refused it. To know that God is gracious and yet not turn from sin in the light of that grace is to fall under God's righteous judgment.

It seems that America is more and more following cults and is involved in the occult. The reason? We know the truth, but we have rejected it. We have rejected God in so many ways in America – taking prayer out of schools, aborting babies, electing officials because of the economy, saying character doesn't count when it comes to elected officials.

America has known the truth but we have rejected it.

Principles to Live By in Daniel 5

Principle #1: **All of us have been weighed and found wanting.** We all have been spiritual lightweights at one time or another. Paul tells us very clearly "…for all have sinned and come short of the glory of God," (Romans 3:23)   and "For the wages of sin is death, (Romans 6:23). When it comes to sin, our days are numbered. Jesus made up for our shortcomings when it comes to sin, through his death on the cross, "but the gift of God is eternal life in Christ Jesus our Lord."

Principle #2: **All people who inherit eternal life do so by grace through faith, not by works.** Ephesians 2:8,9 tells us, "It is by grace you are saved through faith, not by works… How was Belshazzar found "wanting" spiritually? He neglected knowledge he had received. Daniel said to Bel, "You knew all this.   Instead you have set yourself up against the Lord of heaven" (Daniel 5:22-23). He knew about his grandfather's faith – he knew all about it.

Principle #3: **God continues to reach out to all people with His grace, no matter how rebellious and sinful they are.** The handwriting on the wall was a message of doom to Belshazzar, but it was a wake-up call to those 1,000 nobles. They could turn to

Daniel's God and Neb's God. And the message was blazed in the plaster so people could read the message again and again: "Numbered, Numbered, Weighed, Divided." It could happen to you, if you don't turn to God.

Principle #4: **God's patience with sinful humanity is definitely correlated with the way we respond to what we know about His will for our lives.** To know your days are numbered, to know you are a spiritual lightweight in the eyes of God, and to get in the face of God is disastrous. The Hebrews writer warns us: "Today, if you hear His voice, do not harden your hearts..." (Hebrews 3:15).

> *Pride is a spiritual condition in which the heart is in the wrong place.*

Life Application

Bel had a serious heart problem. When a Michigan man entered the hospital for tests, he never would have guessed what the doctors would find. At first they thought the X-ray technicians had put their film in backward. But then they discovered that nothing was wrong with the X-rays. There was something wrong with the patient. The man's heart was in a reversed position. What was supposed to be on the left side of the man's chest was on the right side and vice versa. He had a rare reversed-organ condition. His heart was not where it was supposed to be (Our Daily Bread, 10/17/97).

In Daniel 5 we read of a different kind of heart problem; one that is all too common. This chapter vividly reminds us that pride is a spiritual condition in which the heart is in the wrong place. Both King Nebuchadnezzar and his grandson Belshazzar were told that they had misplaced hearts of arrogance and pride. As a result, God judged them. Nebuchadnezzar was made low until he recognized that the most High God ruled over all (v. 21), and his grandson, Belshazzar, was slain (v. 30).

We need to examine ourselves often to see if our heart is in the right place. Do we depend on God daily? Do we acknowledge that all we have and are is by God's mercy and grace? Do we live as His grateful servants, yielding to His will? Only as we recognize the importance of genuine humility and acknowledge our dependence on Him can we have a heart that's in the right place. Where is your heart?

NOTES

Chapter 6

Staying True No Matter What
Daniel 6:1-28

A pastor friend of mine shared with me about a very dramatic happening in one of the Sunday School classes in his church some time ago. In the class they were discussing the critical question: Is it harder to live for God or to die for God? An elderly gentleman in the class rose to his feet and with real vigor said, "I think it is immensely harder to live for God than it is to die for God." And no sooner had he said that than he fell over dead. Talk about making your point! Dying for God is usually a brief, though possibly intense experience; but living for God is a lifetime commitment.

As we approach Chapter six of Daniel, we need to remember that even as Daniel faces a lion's den for God he had been living for God for 73 years. In those 73 years, from age 17 to age 90, he had been under constant pressure from a pagan society, Babylon, in which he was forced to live day in and day out. He had also been under constant pressure from a pagan kingdom in which he was forced to serve, in top administrative posts, in the very pagan palace of Babylon. Yes, Daniel was going to have to face a lions' den, but remember the devil is called a lion and Daniel had been living in his cage for 70 years. Those who understand this would say he was consistently in a whole lot more danger in Satan's cage than he was in the lions' den of

Babylon. The thing that is going to bring the victory as we live in this spiritually dark world is consistency or commitment and God-given courage. Consistency and commitment are qualities we must give ourselves to today. God-given courage will be apportioned to those who depend upon God's Spirit for help in the crisis of life.

> *The thing that is going to bring victory as we live in this spiritually dark world is consistency and commitment and God-given courage.*

Consistency & Commitment Needed
For Godly Living Today

Daniel 6:1-20

As we consider Daniel's 73 years of life, we have seen tremendous consistency and commitment. The first time we met Daniel in chapter 1, at the ripe old age of 17 years old, we see that he "resolved not to defile himself" when it came to living a godly life (Daniel 1:8). The pagan society and powers that were around him in Babylon tried to get him to compromise his commitment to God. Daniel refused to fall for it or give in to it. As we come to chapter 6 of Daniel we find that at the age of 90 years old, Daniel is still consistent in his character. In verse 3 we see that "Daniel so distinguished himself…by his exceptional qualities that the king planned to set him over the whole kingdom." Daniel not only had seniority, he had superiority. When his enemies tried to find some fault in him concerning his work ethic, they could find "no corruption in him" (v. 4) for he was "trustworthy and neither corrupt nor negligent."

At 90 years old Daniel was still committed in his spiritual life. Talk about commitment to the Lord! In verse 10 we read, "Now when Daniel learned that the decree had been published (knowing the consequences of his action), he went home to his upstairs room where the windows opened toward Jerusalem. Three times a day he got down on his knees and prayed, giving thanks to his God, just as he had done before." Now that's consistency! He had a disciplined prayer life; he prayed three times a day and he had been doing that for probably most of his life. Prayer time included thanksgiving (v. 10) and intercession, as we see in verse 11.

He also served God "continually"; so much so that the pagan emperor, Darius, mentions it two times (vv. 16, 20). He lived his life so straight that he could say to Darius, "I was found innocent in His (God's) sight. Nor have I ever done any wrong before you, O king." (v. 22). In this day of vacillation, with so much political and lifestyle change, there is such a need for consistency and commitment in the lives of believers. Can you be counted on? People look around for stability and common sense in this crazy world and what do they see? Can they see that you are standing on the Solid Rock, Christ Jesus?

What about your prayer life? Would it make any difference in your personal life or in the church if prayer was banned for 30 days? In one region of Africa, the first converts to Christianity were very diligent about praying. In fact, the believers each had their own special place outside the village where they went to pray in solitude. The villagers reached these "prayer rooms" by using their own private footpaths through the brush. When grass began to grow over one of these trails, it was evident that the person to whom it belonged was not praying very much. Because these new Christians were concerned for each other's spiritual welfare, a unique custom sprang up. Whenever anyone noticed an overgrown "prayer path", he or she would go to the person and lovingly warn, "Friend, there's grass on your path." (Our Daily Bread, 11/10/92). What about your prayer life? Is it consistent and is it full of thanksgiving and intercession? We cannot imagine how much is accomplished in our own lives in our world and in the lives of others through prayer.

Do you take a stand when it counts? The world is watching you. Are you up and down in your Christian living? Are you in and out of church? Are you in one church for a few months and then in another for a few months? What can you be counted on for? Where is your consistency? Where is your commitment? Can a struggling believer or unbeliever count on you?

Would it make any difference in your personal life or in your church if prayer was banned in the United States for 30 days?

God-Given Courage Vital for Godly Living

Daniel 6:20-28

The prophet Daniel stands out as a most admirable example of uncompromising and courageous conviction. Someone once said, "When conviction strikes deep enough, courage rises to sustain it." Because the emperor was going to promote Daniel to be the head of the Kingdom, those around him were green-eyed with jealousy. They tried to find something to charge Daniel with to bring him down, but they were unable to do so. You can't keep people from talking about you, but you can so live as to make them liars if they slander you. Daniel was too consistent in trustworthiness and never was involved in corruption of any kind. He also was not negligent.

The consensus was that if they were to find anything to accuse Daniel with it had to be something to do with his religious practices. Playing on Darius' pride, they got him to pass a stupid law that no one could pray to anyone or anything except to Darius for the next 30 days. Darius fell for it and made the decree that could not be changed and if it was broken the one who broke it would be thrown into the lions' den. Sure enough, they caught Daniel praying to God instead of Darius – surprise, surprise!

Darius was distressed that he had been so foolish and tried until sundown to rescue Daniel from the lions' den. We see in this instance that it was better to be a child of faith in a den of lions than a king in a palace without faith. The king was distressed for Daniel. According to verse 14 he spent the whole night without sleep. While Darius agonized, however, Daniel was delivered from the lions by an angel.

With the first light of dawn the king hurried to the lions'
den and called to Daniel in an anguished voice, "Daniel,
servant of the living God, has your God, whom you serve
continually, been able to rescue you from the lions?" (v.
20). Daniel calls back that God kept him from being hurt
and they found no wounds on him because "he had trusted
in God" (v. 23).

> *When conviction strikes*
> *deep enough, courage rises*
> *to sustain it.*

Dare to be a Daniel

One of the outstanding Bible teachers of the past century, C.I. Scofield, often told of an incident that helped believers find deliverance from their sins and their evil habits. He said, "Shortly after I was saved, I passed by the window of a store in St. Louis where I saw on display a painting of Daniel in the lions' den. That great man of faith, with his hands behind his back and those wild beasts circling him, was looking up and answering the king who was anxious to know if God had protected him from physical harm." Scofield continued, "As I stood there, great courage and hope flooded my heart. Only a few days had passed since I, a drunken lawyer, had been converted; and no one had yet told me anything about the keeping power of Jesus Christ. I thought to myself, there are lions all about me too, such as my old habits and sins. But the One who shut the mouths of lions for Daniel can also shut them for me! I knew that I could not win the battle in my own strength. The painting made me realize that while I was weak and helpless, my God was strong and able. He had saved me, and now He would also be able to deliver me from the wild beasts in my life. Oh what a rest of spirit that truth brought to me!" (Our Daily Bread, 10/24/76).

To rely on our own willpower when we are confronted with challenges and hard places in our lives is to court defeat. But if we give the Holy Spirit day by day control of our lives, we will experience a wonderful surge of power and courage in our lives. The God who delivered Daniel can also do the same for any of His children who put their trust in Him. The power of the Spirit can give us the courage to live the Godly life. This is the only way we can stay true no matter what.

Life Application

Spiritual victory will come as we live consistent and committed lives through the courage given by the Holy Spirit. As Daniel comes to the close of His life, he experiences wonderful victory. His enemies are defeated (v. 24). The Lord is glorified through King Darius' witness – look at how Darius glorifies the Lord because of Daniel's consistency, commitment, and great courage. He proclaims that the God of Daniel "Is the living God and He endures forever; His kingdom will not be destroyed, His dominion will never end..."(v. 26). The kingdoms of this world will end, but not the Kingdom of God. Daniel's God also "rescues and He saves; He performs signs and wonders in the heavens and on the earth." (v. 27). Darius had seen this before his very eyes on this day.

And Daniel prospered, even throughout his old age (v. 28). You talk about victory! Do you long for Victory in your spiritual life? It won't come easy or quickly. It takes consistency and commitment over the long haul: day-by-day faithfulness to God and Godly things no matter what. It takes God-given courage to take a stand for God by the help of the Holy Spirit. This saying is so true: Courage is fear that has said its prayers.

Will you take a stand for your Lord where you live and work and go to school? God is looking for people who will stay true to Him and His cause in today's world. He's looking for young and old alike to give themselves to living the Christian life day in and day out, year after year, come what may. Sunshine or rain, easy or hard, they are com-mitted and seek God's help to have courage to stay true to the end. God can make us that kind of people as we give ourselves to Him.

NOTES

Bibliography

Preaching Today , PreachingToday.com, Tape #98.
   Cassette.

Stanley, Andy, *Visioneering,* Sisters, Oregon,
   Multnomah Publishers, 1999.

Tan, Paul Lee, *Encyclopedia of 7,700 Illustrations,* Bible
   Communications, 1979

The Daily Bread, Grand Rapids Michigan, Radio Bible
   Class, May 23, 1969, March 22, 1971, October 24,
   1976, January 1, 1992, April 6, 1992,November 10,
   1992, and October 17, 1997.

ABOUT THE AUTHORS:

Rev. Frank Beck is the senior pastor at Gates Wesleyan Church. He's been a pastor for over forty years in various churches and has been at Gates Wesleyan for the past twenty five years. Frank lives in Gates, New York, a suburb of Rochester, with his wife Zelma.

~*~

Patricia Chadwick is a freelance writer and publisher of two online magazines. History's Women highlights the extraordinary achievements of women throughout history. A stay-at-home mom for sixteen years, Patti also publishes Parents & Teens, an online magazine geared to help parents connect with their teens. Visit her sites at www.historyswomen.com and www.parentsandteens.com. She lives in Batavia, New York, with her husband John and her three wonderful teens, T.J., Jeni, and David.

CONTACT INFORMATION:

Email: Daniel@pcpublicaitons.org

Website: http://www.pcpublications.org

To order additional copies of

TAKING A STAND

Send $9.95 plus $2.00
shipping and handling to:

PC Publications
22 Williams St.
Batavia, NY 14020

For credit card orders visit:
http://www.PCPublications.org
or call (585)343-2810

*Quantity discounts available.
Send inquiries to:
Daniel@PCPublications.org

OTHER TITLES
BY P.C. PUBLICATIONS

HISTORY'S WOMEN – THE UNSUNG HEROINES
Available at: www.historyswomen.com

ebook: $ 5.95
print: $15.95

~*~

RENEWING THE HEART
A 30-Day Devotional Journal for Parents of Teens
Available at: www.parentsandteens.com

Ebook - $3.95
Print - $6.95

~*~

LOOK UP
A 30-Day Devotional Journal for Teens
Available at : www.parentsandteens.com

Ebook - $3.95
Print - $6.95

MISSION POSSIBLE: RAISING GREAT TEENS!
A realistic guide to raising up your teens.
Available at: www.parentsandteens.com

Ebook - $5.95
Print   - $12.95

~*~

HAPPY HOLIDAYS WITH TEENS
Traditions, recipes, and gifts teens will love.

Ebook - $ 7.95
Print: - $11.95

~*~

THE COMPLETE GUIDE TO PASTORAL VISITATION
An indepth look at both lay and pastoral visitation.

Ebook - $6.95
Print   - $16.95

To order visit http://www.pcpublications.org or contact the
publisher at books@pcpublicaitons.org